# Drawing on Memory

# Drawing on Memory

Tom Conaty

REVIVAL PRESS

LIMERICK - IRELAND

Copyright © Tom Conaty 2022

First published in Ireland by
Revival Press
Limerick, Ireland

Revival Press is the poetry imprint of
The Limerick Writers' Centre
c/o The Umbrella Project, 78 O'Connell Street,
Limerick, Ireland

www.limerickwriterscentre.com
www.facebook.com/limerickwriterscentre

Book Design and Typesetting: Lotte Bender (www.pamalottestudios.com)
Cover Image: *Liminal Landscape*, Emma Finucane
Managing Editor Revival Press: Dominic Taylor

ISBN    978-1-7396183-0-8

A CIP catalogue number for this publication is available from The British Library

We acknowledge the support of The Limerick Writers' Centre Community Publishing
Project

*for Kim*

*for Davin and Finn*

*and for all my family,
here and gone*

*in memory of Jac Veale*

Memory, daughter of Heaven and Earth,
and Mother of The Nine Muses.

'The past beats inside me like a second heart'
— John Banville, *The Sea*.

Memory
One had a lovely face,
And two or three had charm,
But charm and face were in vain
Because the mountain grass
Cannot but keep the form
Where the mountain hare has lain.
— W.B. Yeats

# CONTENTS

## Making A Mark

## The Cartographer's Hand

## Borderline

## Truth Lies Here

**Scars On The Land**

**Drawing Up A List Of Nouns – The Names For Love**

# MAKING A MARK

# Both Sides

And who am I,
when I'm at home?

And who am I,
when I'm away?

The answer lies
in neither
but both –

the settled
and the stray.

## Night Light

Moon, hold your ground.
Don't listen to the sun who,
for too long, has fallen in love
with its own light.

And the tide of opinion is with you,
in that you pull your own weight
and more, in a firmament
that points too much to stars
to come home by.

## BREATH

phonemes,
smallest units of sound,

fricatives,
either side of a double vowel
one voiced, one voiceless –

breath,

first thing in the morning when I wake,
I hear you,

last thing at night
slipping away,

before I fall asleep.

## The Intruder

The intruder
came again last night,
in through my
up-and-down sash window.

Velveting her way around
my every room,
left with a ring,
a band of gold,
a time piece,

chime of hours
around my days
and a necklace,

string of pearly beads
to reel me in again.

# There It Is, Gone

That lost poem, you know the one,
the one you had this morning,
in your head before you awoke,
the one you were sure would be there
when you opened your eyes,
has gone missing now,
without a trace.

I have sent out word to all my contacts,
put posters up on bus shelters,
simulated the event on camera,
checked cctv footage for scansion.

Nothing of significance has emerged,
no line of enquiry from the Gardaí,
they have nothing to go on.
Word has it
that similar events have been reported.

A pattern is emerging.
The victim's guard is generally down,
someone or something comes calling,
knocking on the door.

The door is usually off the latch
or they have a key.
They seem familiar and
what they have to say is familiar too,
even when it sounds strange.

You find yourself repeating
what they said so often,
that you are convinced
it is you that is speaking.

It can be accompanied by images,
though not always.
The reel or spool is played
over and over again.
You turn in the bed,
reach for a pen,
house lights come up and
there it is,

gone.

## COPYRIGHT

No, I wasn't looking over her shoulder
at what she was writing,
I was looking out the window
at the river below,
into the distance, the way
the master taught us in school,

out to where the lily lies,
concave, white flower, nestling on top,
bobbing and swaying from side to side,
yet anchored to the riverbed
by a stem of scapular green,
going downwards.

Yet when we look to examine
how it holds,
we see our faces,
mirrored back –
smooth, then wrinkled
in the ripple of the river run...

So the fact that
my poem
resembles hers in some way,
has nothing to do with me copying
but more to do
with our point of view –

more to do with the fact that
we were looking out the same window.

## DUET ON A MANUSCRIPT

*dexter and sinister, light and shade,*
*together, show us how the world is made*

The right hand writes the right thing down,
joins up all the dots of knowing
how to have everything in place,
each curve, each upstroke, downstroke, each space.

All horizontal, vertical, oblique lines
parallel, and corralled within the confines
of red for upper,
blue for lower case.

Then along comes the 'ciotóg', the left hand,
like a drunk at a family do,
staggering all over the room, the page,
a spidery weave, breaking out of the cage

of signature script. No distinctive mark
but lightly dancing like a Dervish, whirling,
shading over the given word, the work,
with the glossolalia, dysgraphia of it all.


'Mc Cafferty, what's this we have
from your scriptorium today?
Would you look at it,
a ball of wool, the cat got at.'

# Lucky The Cat

Cranking up the spine, after sleep,
old tomcat eases himself into the day,

opens his mouth, outstretched paw
fanning talons, a feline claw

of breakneck grip, sharpening up
the daytime for a night time routine,

when sleep falls upon the world,
like a drooping eyelid blanket of black.

The owner's hand under his belly
lifts the U-bend.

The backdoor opens,
release, a fall to earth –

cushioned drop,
a shiver on landing,

into a swagger,
old Lucky, the tomcat,

travels light
silent tremor of the night.

## FREEDOM OF SPEECH
*for Lily*

How was Lily, the Golden Retriever, to know
that barking was not allowed in suburbia and
that there was an absolute curfew on freedom of
expression between dusk and dawn?

Come on, she thought, can a dog of my age not
have the liberty to clear her throat,
respond to that mutt next door,
who seems to get away with murder?

And what else do they expect me to do with
those fuckin' magpies? (sorry)
count them?
Gimmie a break.

Ah Jaysus,
You've no idea what it's like.
If I attempt the slightest wuff
you have our fella, out the door

like a shot, with a muzzle in his hand
barking at me
and the big long quizzical head
of the muppet next door,

straining across the fence,
tut tutting.
Ah hello!

I wouldn't mind it but
I was inside the house the other night
and our fella and his lovely missus
were having a bit of a barney.

It came to a stage where she had
enough of his argumentativeness and
she told him to keep quiet.

Well you should have seen the face of him.

## First Thing This Morning

"a little silver slipper of a moon",
the north star,
a dark December sky,

out the back door of hope,
to a garden of green grass,
bare trees, turning in on themselves,

inhaling hibernation,
holding breath.

I exhale,
let the dog out,
lift the incontinence pads,
for ageing Retrievers,
off the kitchen floor.

Like yesterday,
me and Lily are turning up
for another day.

We'll hang around,
'til we have
a full moon to howl at.

## BACKWOODSMAN

He is no Red Branch knight, this morning,
in these woods.

No lithe warrior stride,
twigs break under his feet.

A sciatic nerve holds back bending
under the arch of leaning boughs.

In a watering hole, he catches
a glimpse of himself.

He sucks in the years,
stands bolt upright, straight,

three ivy strings
hang from a tree.

He weaves their tiara pull
into a single garland,

lets it rest on his head, confers upon himself
the majesty of woods,

the interiority of trees,
the strangeness of paths

and the beguiling
intimacy of shortcuts home.

Behind him he leaves a hanging crown,
in shafts of wood light,

for the next passer-by,
the next pretender to the throne.

# THE RELUCTANT SHOPKEEPER

Never worked a till her whole life,
more a box she slipped out from
underneath the counter.

Wooden, and smooth,
with the hand shine of pushed in,
pulled out, all those years
since he left,

that nestled on the apron,
on her knees as she sat
on a high stool,
serving the regulars.

Economy of movement, the key.
Everything within arm's reach,
in the bits and pieces –
neighbourhood-kind of shop we all need,

to keep the show on the road,
feel the intimacy of exchange.
And each customer to their own items
and more off a shelf

or out of the one fridge,
onto the counter.
Then the accustomed dialogue to follow:
'Is that everything?'

'It is I think, until I get home.

Then the hand-plunge into the pocket
for coins, the lift out and scatter.

'Do you mind taking this stuff'?

'All the same to me;
it's all money, isn't it?'

Then the practiced scan.

'Wait till we see what we have here'.

And the arthritic fingers on the right hand,
index and middle,
flicking denominations of ten cents, twenties, fifties
into the free hand that funnelled, disappeared,
then surfaced again with neat euro piles.

She'd do the hard sums in her head,
then double checked the damage
with pen and paper,
ball-pointing each step along the lines of units, tens
and the usual carry on into the hundreds, the euros.

Totals totted on two calculators,
then partitioning
the spoils on the counter,
she would add:

'That's for you and this is for me.
That's it'.

'Thank you'.

'Thank you'.

Open door,
then shut.

Each time she would tumble the towers,
with her palms,
into an opening drawer.

She fumbled in the makeshift till,
sensing still in her finger tips
the desire to sort out, rearrange,
the cold unyielding,
hard currency of change.

DRAWING ON MEMORY

## Waiting Room

**1.**

I could think of better pages to have open
in the A&E department, I know,
than the Death Notices.

I scan today's arrivals, wonder if I,
like them, will die in alphabetical order,
cause no fuss, take the medicine,
when my time comes.

One, gone, after a long illness, one suddenly,
another, in the wonderful care of the hospice,
a little one,  Abigail, died on arrival,
scarcely seen the light of day.

We gather in our grief, consign it
to a top shelf, out of sight.
We wrap it up in time.

And in no time now the triage nurse
will call me up, determine what time, if any,
I have left, to count, in this pinball arcade
of lined-up fruits, jackpots,
spent coins.

**2.**

I know it must have been a mistake,
a typo, a faux pas,
call it what you will, that day in admissions,
when the clerical officer, behind her perspex panel,
having taken my details and those of next of kin,
nonchalantly enquired: 'have you gone for your autopsy yet?'

When she received no immediate reply
she took it to mean not applicable
and duly ticked the appropriate box.
I asked for clarification.
She asked me to take a seat.
And, as if swatting away an irksome fly,
on to the next thing,       Ding,   she informed me
that the Consultant would explain everything.

**3.**

The sun shone through a ceanothus,
creeping on a climbing frame,
outside the waiting-room window,
casting a lattice of lines, intersecting shadows,
on the white pages of my open journal.

## SHADOW BOXING
*a contender for his own crown*

Against the ropes,
against himself,
he is blue corner and red
in one.

Southpaw, northpaw,
taking the body blows
that will bring him down.

Fissure and tear,
the waning desire,
to rise again
and face the count.

Down on the spattered canvas,
where the artist's knife
has left its mark.

# THE CARTOGRAPHER'S HAND

# Elusive

**1.**

The cartographer's hand
is pawing at the silence
on an old road,

at the high hedges
that filter sunlight;
hold the darkness.

The stillness sings
the only song of here and now
and the faltering breath of it all.

**2.**

We search, we fumble
in the out-house of discarded things,
unsure what to rescue,
reuse, let go.

**3.**

And where did I go all these years,
decades, straddling millennia?
I cast my lot with the cast of the fisherman.
Take me to where the river flows.

## Field Notes

*In response to 'In the Current' by Yvonne Cullivan,*
*a Public Art Project based in Belturbet, County Cavan*

### Part 1

Memory,
       is snagged on bushes,
       on overhanging trees,
       when waters recede.

Secrets,
       are written in many tongues.
       We go by word of mouth
       and the mouth of the river

       opens all.

### Béal Tairbirt

Béal Tairbirt ag oscailt
ar shlí na habhann,
ag sní,

idir doiléireacht na gcoillte is
fairsinge mhór an ghoirt.

Sólás na hoíche,
scáth na maidine,
ar bheola gach aon ní

atá a nochtadh,

ar bheola gach aon ní
atá fé cheilt.

## Belturbet

The mouth of Turbet opening
to the way of the river,
flowing,

through the darkness of the wood,
the wide and open field.

Consolation of night,
shadow of morning,
on the lips of everything

being revealed,
on the lips of everything,
hidden away.


There are places
you have never seen,
that lie in waiting,
in places you have been before

and thought you knew.

## Arrival

Talk was of straight lines,
from A to B
in no time,
bypass the byword.

Engineers theodolited their way
through trees and fields,
plotted the camber and the fall,
the dunt of the hard shoulder to the sheugh.

Right angles looked awkward,
horizontal lines  too flat,
vertical ones had the whiff
of too much ascension,

oblique lines
made everything clear.

And so the mapmaker came
when the earth was turning,
when new roads around the town
were being laid down.

She wore a satchel.
Instruments were sharpened.
She had precision in mind,

a compass to point the way,
a mirror to see things
reflected back.

She had intent in her eyes.
With a pencil
she was taking things down:

the overhang of a tree,
a market house that had lost its name,
the hand that fed the weights to the scales,

that found fungus on the forest floor,
separated curds and whey,
spilt salt.

She pencilled in the shade of alleyways,
that had not seen the light of day,
children at play on a fair green.

There's a parchment buried deep
and on it a song,
the songbirds sing.

DRAWING ON MEMORY

Clay under her fingernails
from uncovering layers.
The foundations of the town
had to be found
and they lay under her feet.

## Putiaghans

Scratch of flintstone,
spark-enkíndled straw,
wildfire run and smoke,
twiglight, logburn,
ember red, meat crackling crisp,

they ate around fires like these.

They came through the woods –
alder and oak,
saw the light of day,
in a clearing they made
next to where the river flows.

They wrote down our names
as next of kin,
in their wills they left pathways,
hidden in clay.

The Putiaghans rise,
they're on the march again,
scars of earthmovers on their foreheads
and salt for ever in their hands.

You sleep deeply,
oh cradled ones,
in the folds of hills,
the roots of trees.

You drool at the mouth,
a river of fish,
dorsal and fin,
lightning rod in moonshine.

Your complexion,
under this patina of peat,
is bone deep.

Squelch in the marsh,
a quaking scraw,

the dry rattle of reeds
in the wind, like the wailing

of women who heard you cry,
then consecrated your fields
with salt in their hands,
tears from the sky.


The mapmaker had river water in her hands,
the sound of lapping water on her tongue,
frothing at the edge,
to willow music in the wind,

swan-song white to the flap and wing-beat
rhythm of butterfly, dragonfly,
mayfly on the whip-crack-away
cast of fishermen

into a slow frame, scribbling the air,
a snake-flight line
left to straighten
and right itself,

on the ripple of the river run...

Hands hold
the stains of pollen,
a rainbow bruise
from gathering in
the names of flowers.

And pushing through
when words for flowers were withering,
the benediction of common weeds.

## The Benediction of Common Weeds

The mapmaker carried the names
of common weeds with her,
everywhere,

she wore
black bindweed, black nightshade,

spoke of
fool's parsley and scarlet pimpernel,

she weaved
ground ivy, creeping soft grass,
creeping thistle around her wrist.

Scented and scentless mayweed,
stinking camomile, she kept
in a jar by the door.

She drank the hemlock.

On her head a scarf
of white campion, white clover.
Winter wild oats in her hair,
in her eyes,
volunteer oilseed rape.

She remembered the forget-me-not,

and next to her heart,
in a locket around her neck,
self-heal for safe keeping.


Fields stretched out before her.
Ditches lay down and
she could see
the lie of the land:


how otters build,
badgers and foxes tunnel,
how rabbits open networks,
hares form.

She pointed this out to road makers.
Swifts sped past,
feeding on the wing.
Crows and ravens used the fly-over

on the way home.

* The Lie of the Land that follows is i.m. of Geraldine O'Reilly and Patrick Stanley
who were killed in The Belturbet Bombing on 28th Dec 1972, and Emily and
Tommy Bullock, and Sam Donegan who were killed in the same year and i.m.of all
who died during The Troubles.

PART 2

## The Lie of the Land*

The circuity of water
　　　　　　and the flood,
the meander of cows.
Old roads twist and turn
to the hum of hollow and hill,
that rise and fall
through a patchwork of fields.

The whitethorn blazes a trail,

the maring ditch,
the marching drain,
hold the plot.

Drumlines are written on these hills,
they beat the submission of choked light,
rainfall,　　glugging into glar.

No one can name the sapling now
on the river bank,
they forgot to record the elder's name
before they came and cut it down,
to beat
a path to the water's edge,
for tourist feet.

Trees shade and shawl,
silhouettes fall
in the meadow marsh.

If only we could see
in this watery land,

escaping to higher ground is harder
when the hills seem far away.

## 'You are Here'

The 'you are here'
mark of location on the Diamond map,
is under perspex
and clouded over now from heavy weather
and too many fingers pointing the way.

Who are you,
who stands beside me now?
What colour from the palette
do you choose?

And when the layers are scraped
and blow-torched away,
what colour, then, lies beneath?

For you and I sing dumb
about our true colours.

We wear flamboyant clothes,
fatigues, camouflages and
the red seeps through.

Clay holds The Bloody Pass,
water washes it down and
the red seeps through,
a menstruation of light
through stained glass windows
of high and low churches,
where people at prayer in different pews,
hold rosary beads, books of common prayer
as touchstones,
to the glorious and sorrowful mysteries
of a town, on a river,
flowing north,
across a border,
to the sea.

The Boundary Commission drew
a dividing line through water,
the river runs on…

Your chalice and monstrance
host the same lamb
to the slaughter.

Declarations,
exhortations and
your finger-pointing blame;
when it comes to salvation,
your semtex smells the same.

The cartographer maps the heavy air,
divines water that flows,
keeps the fire, that detonates and blasts,
that rings out in volleys.

She sees past
the empty cartridges and magazines,
spent bullet points in the tired tales
of this borderland.


**Routes**

In the Big Houses on The Lawn
they traced their way by hand
along the wainscot rail,
embossed braille on wallpaper.

Escape routes opened
through fake history books
on bogus shelving,

routes that become roads,
bringing us back to
what we are running from.

She sets the set-square down
in the middle of the town,
opens cat's-eyes on Main Street
for all of us to see.

The 'sorry for your troubles'
shakes the severed hand,
that points the way
through rubble and ruin,

severed branches of a tree
lie in broken masonry.

A north wind blows,
dusts down broken limbs.

The spine arches, uncoils,
the cranium lifts the heavy weight,
radius and ulna take up the hand,
bring the patella to bend
and stand once more.

Achilles stretches,
marches on.
Pounding hearts pulse,
the red weeps, seeps through,
pushes the needle on the compass
to its very limits,
to reveal – True North

and everything else is relative.


New bridges were borne in mind.
Old ones, that had taken the blows,
were given the all clear again,
for weight bearing

but never opened for long.

She set her eyes
to the eyes of the bridge,
that were blown away.
Neighbours waved across the water,
their salutations drowned out
by tourist boats revving-up.

Inflections and stresses
in their speech became more distinct,
more pronounced.

They had to take
the long way round now.
Some chose the short circuit;
out.


In the only eye of the bridge left,
Simon sat. You know the one,
who helped with the cross,
who manned the boat,
when fishermen slept.

Up and down the river, all day,
he carried the sorrow –

*O'Reilly, Geraldine*
*Stanley, Patrick*

that blood red sorrow that seeped
through his veins –

*Emily & Tommy, Bullock*

that blood red grief that seeped
through this remembering
and forgetting land –

*Donegan, Sam*

He stands with them in a rowing boat,
listing, from side to side,
the names of the dead.

When the corncrake forgot about being extinct,
he opened his voice in a singing field.
Song burst from the river,
the kingfisher hovered high.

Levitation was in the air.

Crow remembered that black notes
were on the scale too.

They got the carriage moving again.
Down the track it shunted,
over and back, over and back,
on old sleepers.


The mapmaker left when grass was long,
clocks stole a march on time,
waving winter time goodbye.

The mayfly was up, fish arced,
trees, heavy with leaves, stooped,
drank in the river stream.

The horse chestnut had sent chandeliers
of uplighting from its boughs
and between it and the sunlight
of the morning
the sky took on a reddish hue,

and shepherds remained silent.

# Underwriter*

*for Seamus Heaney*

**1.**

The wind took the house by storm,
no warning was given,
it buffeted every locked window and door,
wheezed through every fissure it could find,
left a landing light without a shade,
swinging to and fro.

The flood is up and with it
grief.
Holding in, gives way to release,
release to breaking
and breaking to waters bursting lamentation
on watermark and watercourse.

The march drain has disappeared,
the path to the river gone.
Paling posts and fence lose
their meaning to the flood.
Barbed wire, blunt from the water's edge.

**2.**

Gone,
his lean-to countryman's step,
moving lightly.

At the bottom of the stairs,
after a reading one night,
'Night men', his words,
on springing off
the last step
of the last flight.
'Night men', he said
before heading out 'into the dark'.

**3.**

That place,
where you have gone so many times;
'the sky at the bottom of the well',
where you move 'into the marvellous'.

Is that where you are now?
Some say they saw you
on stepping stones
crossing the river Styx,
making your own way.

The ferryman waved you on.

*Elbow and chanter of lament*
*and the gravelly cello bow*
*play you down, underground,*
*past Antaeus wrestling,*
*Hercules, coming up for air*
*lifting you,*
*your limbs earthing the sky.*

**4.**

Whose borders are we crossing?
The 'you-are-here mark' of location
has been taken away.
Are we supposed to know the histories?
the geographers made in water and clay.

The day you died,
words were on the run,
in search of safe houses,
underground.

Crumble to tilth
and leach,
the syntax of silence sings
souterrain songs
that seep down
to your perfect pitch.

**5.**

You are underwriter now,
dismantle all,
decompose.

Sing us, to 'where the singing comes from',
underscore your requiem,
with parts for the next internees.

*Written for the lost Quarterman Manuscript of poems in Tribute to Seamus
Heaney

# BORDERLINE

## STRAND LINES

Every line you draw divides directions,
it's an arbitrary line
you lay.
Next time you feel the inclination,
inscribe it in sand,
so the sea may wash it away.

# Burying The Compass

**1.**

The further north we go,
the more south insists
on opening up behind us.

And south, in its turn,
will give way to north.

East and west,
an arm on a cross,
word coming in
from all directions.

**2.**

So how can we bury the compass?
How can we tell the north to close its mouth?
Stop the north star shining.

Or say to the south –
'stay warm and all will be well'.

Or to the west- 'stop bringing us, always,
to the edge of things'.

And how can we say to the east –
that beginning again is totally out of the question?

## SOOTHSAYER LIGHT

The woman, with voices in her head,
has one eye that she can see with,
the other, the closed one,
she leaves for vision.

Discarded, darkened iris,
flower of underworld and over,
milky white,
with soothsayer's light,
looking into the beyond,

of the present, a past,
the prophesy of every last thing
– a last breath,
last arc of a hand,
turn of a head,
the rise and fall
of a heaving chest.

Intake and release.

In a swirling wind,
a dying air sings
the eyelids closed,
and the one eye,
closed off in its darkness,

peers through me, enquires,

have I seen the border fox
of late.

## A Border Fox

Nocturnal time takes the dark to heart,
swallows the penumbra
of the wood,

black clouds keep the bell silent,
the call to prayer, the crunch
on gravel, when lights go out.

Dark night that holds
the furtive kiss,
the lovemaking, in white,
near a sepulchre of bones.

A hand lifts the baton
on a bandstand, where players
have left flutes, oboes, the cor anglais
to prevailing winds,

to sing a song of hollow and reed.

And on the road between the dark brae
and the white bridge,
a border fox is listening,
out at this ungodly hour,
listening.

# Knowing The Boundaries

Street lights at the end of the village
dim and fade,
yield to the dark wood.

The known path, not easy to find,
when the known tree and hedge
silhouette against the wintering sky,

mesh with the macabre,
leaving hand touch and footfall
to do the seeing,

the inner ear to sense
the terror of the vixen's
lonely cry of love,

the crow's inebriated caw
and the badger's nocturnal habit
of seeing, watching everything,
in black and white.

We make our way on a road, following
a continuous white line,
where nothing,
no one, is supposed to pass.

# Truth Lies Here

## THE WAITING GAME

You are looking for portents,
for signs, a dedicated time,
when everything aligns
and someone comes calling

across this reluctant, stuttering,
stammering place of; not now,
where tongue ties knots in words,
yet words, in torrents come spilling

from your mouth in ancient rhyme,
remembered verses, by heart;
Elliot's 'Prufrock', your favourite,
the gauntlet – 'Do I dare…'

Mary's Webb, from your mother's lips,
lulling in your ears
and a Jethro Tull lyric – 'on Preston platform'…
'moves the ground under you'

and me as we circle our favourites.
The river Teme, in Ludlow now
is 'within earshot' of both of us,
Heaney's 'Beech Grove,'a stone's throw away

in a garden of a neighbour you met,
by chance one day, when you threw open
your doors to the street and
let the voices in,

to fill your rooms.
When you're alone you take down
a copy of Houseman's Collected
and from the collected, you select

'The First of May,' your birthday.
You read it with delight
like an omen, a seal of approval,
stamped on your forehead.

Reluctantly you open
closed notebooks.
Entries surprise you.
mildly detonate…

Now is the time to make hay,
harvest the windfalls.

The wizard, your four-sided bookcase,
turns in your living room.
Your books, back from storage,
show us their spines again.

## Opening Night At The Exhibition

Out beyond seeing,
far beyond hearing, listening,
way out past touch, taste and smell
lies an eye,
an ear,
a tongue,
a nose for what is beautiful.

A scent in the gallery
of the bespoke,
the unsaid,
the unheard,
the undone.

Curator and curated
stand side by side
and the doors at the exhibition
are about to open.

## APPETITE

Do all the muscles employed
to create that fake smile of yours
know that they have been recruited,
frogmarched for deception?

Do the nerve endings and sensilla
on your palm have any idea
that the handshake closed on
a treacherous deal?

What of your feet when
they walked away?
Your ears when they heard
the lie?

And your lips,
your wonderous lips,
what tongue whets
your appetite now?

## Whose Hands Are These

Whose hands are these that move the pieces?
And what game is it, that's being played
out around this chequered board?

Whose hands are these,
adding weights to the scales,
tilting the balance in favour of down?

Cupped together,
whose hands are drinking
leaky water, from the stream?

And what of the one,
fan like, hiding his mouth,
sparing us the mastication of lies?

## Say No More

In the lecture hall of his own mouth,
his exuberant tongue luxuriated
in his own words.
A swagger to accompany,
a strut, a mock-sincere tilted head,
and a boom that spilt chapter and verse words
over the lectern, the pulpit, the altar,
splattering the congregation of the faith,
who sat in pews,
listening to the good news,
that some found hard to swallow.

## Lasting Impression

The shoemaker's son went
barefoot.

Sole leather in his father's hand,
the spit of his son's step,
an impression on a last,

that another would wear
threadbare,

and bring back to him,
his father's heir
to reheel,

repair.

## Contamination

In his capacity as chaplain to St. Patrick's Hospital,
Fr. Boyle informed everyone, with a heavy heart,
that the sprinkling of holy water,
in operating theatres and wards,
would be discontinued.
This was a measure, he said,
imposed by Health and Safety,
to curb the spread of infection.

# BREAKING THE BREAD OF LIFE – A COMMUNION SEQUENCE

## I

### What if, Pontiff
*(after Raymond Carver)*

What if, pontiff, I were to say –
summer,
whisper the soft white petal of the mayflower
in your ear,
the plucked flower in her tiny hand –
frozen?

And what if your disciple comes over all big and black,
on his white marble throne
and the halo of his big-black shoeshine
extinguishes the sanctuary lamp?
What then pontiff, what then,
when the candlewick flame is snuffed out?

Stale breath, soutane and stole lean towards her,
the hands that stalked her, staked her
with the crucifix,
now hold the host –
"take this all of you and eat it,
this is my body", (he says).

And what if, pontiff, I were to say
that she takes it time and time again
and in her communion reflection
she prays wailing and crying into the time…
if only, if only,
if only a thousand times.

A requiem rises inside her little heart,
to comfort the crying:

*Stabat mater dolorosa,*
*O quam tristis et afflicta,*
*miserere, miserere, miserere*
a breakout cry of *libera me.*
a Calvary cry of
*Eloi, Eloi lama sabachthani?*
My God, my God,
why have you forsaken me?
Forsaken me and all alone.

Meanwhile,
back at the church.

The principal takes to the lectern,
informs everybody that this year's Communion
has been bigger and better than ever.
"A big *go raibh maith agat* to Bean Uí Luanaigh for preparing
the children so well and
an even bigger *bualadh bos* for Fr. Boyle for giving us
this beautiful ceremony here today.
I know we won't forget it and
I know the children won't forget it either."

And what if, pontiff, I were to say (very quietly)
that the day dissolves into tokens of words,
coins pressed into the hand for forgetting
and the muffled sound of the man himself's voice singing,
after tea and biscuits in the school,
the muffled sound that she can hear almost forty years later.

Oh, and he could sing all right, pontiff, note perfect;
lips protruding, hips cocked and collar up, as if he were Elvis,
three or four verses of 'I'm All Shook Up' and everyone would join in;
"I'm all shook up, huh huh huh, huh huh huh, yeah yeah."

One thing everyone agreed upon was that Fr. Boyle
was a great man to give you a laugh, that's for sure,
you were always guaranteed a good laugh if he were around.

## II

### Runway

Gate B21 opened its mouth
on a gaping runway,
that roared of departures.

The air hostess tilted her head
sideways, her welcome-aboard smile
could not conceal

her pity for the young woman,
who had rainfall, storm,
written on her face.

The on-board magazine, *Cara*,
promised the comfort of *Avoca* food
the warmth of a *Foxford* rug – perfume…

The seating arrangement was open,
she chose a place right next
to the emergency exit.

## III

### Screech

On Brighton Pier,
a gull screeched over her head.

Dead eyeing each other,
they vied for tourist bread.

**IV**

**Deadly Nightshade**
*(they had to bury him somewhere)*

That night the hedges were fluorescent
with the bright yellow arc of headlights,
the cars, in the cortége, sirened
on back roads, outriders for the hearse,
that sped to the Abbey, hours past midnight
for the burial, in camera,
in obscura.

No chief mourners,
no pall bearers, no order of carriage,
no flowers, no notice for "no flowers",
no scraps of paper for the eulogy,
no eulogy,
no mention of ordination,
no silver or golden jubilation,
no one to say, 'sorry for your troubles',
no one to say it to ...

He was buried in the dark
of deadly nightshade,
in ready-mixed Norbertine clay.

Badger turned out as mother superior,
magpies were young novitiates,
crows and ravens wore vestments of the dead
and starlings were totally out of order,
mimicking, mocking the last rites instead.

# V

## Canon Law

At the Congregation to codify
Canon law,
verbs for love were taken out,
and an overwhelming majority voted
in favour of dropping nouns,
on the basis that
they named things.

# UNSEEN

**1.**

Crow of cock,
bellow bull
and the steamy phalanx of
Friesians at an outhouse door,
steaming up the frostbite,
throatbite-steamy morning air.

The heave and hunch of haunch
against each other for the heat,
flood gates of hot white piss,
streaming down underneath the herd melody,
of hoof scratch and scrape
on frozen-cow dung spoor.

Free fall of skitter scutter,
slap on dimpled concrete,
urethra of urine wash and
the yell of yellow into pavement cracks…

Opened her senses to the white stained sheet
and the ice fields.

Once more to the shit heap of this farmyard,
no yard brush or squeegee could squeeze clean…

**2.**

Next would come the plaintive wail –

'Is there none of ye can take them cattle
down to the new land?'

'The none of ye' was her,
she knew.

She volunteered, most times,
and in her bright new dress and
red buckled shoes,

she sidestepped
the excrement of the herd,
on a wide open country road,

for everyone to see.

# Pigs Suite

## 1.

### Pigging

My mother reared pigs by hand,
big landrace pigs, under
the colour, heat and light
of an infrared bulb.

Metal crate,
big sow on her side,
teats falling to the ground,
heavy with  milk.

Nudging, climbing one over
the other, butting and voraciously
chomping, leaky milk,
side snouting on to straw.

Brushes of bristle
on bony backs,
opening and rising,
feed after feed.

## 2.

### Dressing the Pigs

Smith, of the penknife flick
and metal-back Wilkinson's Sword
blade between
the lips,

cut a line between two humps
under the skin,
slit and scooped
mercury balls onto a metal plate,

sluiced them into a metal bucket,
then onto a dunghill
and the balls, jelly like,
in testicular light,

catch the eye of the magpie,
who pulls and teases
the delicate muscularity
apart.

'One for sorrow,
Two for joy', skywards,
'dressing the pigs',
dressing their nests.

### 3.

### The Crow Brady

Brady, the pig dealer
enters the yard.
Big leathery back, big leathery black
boots, elasticated at the side.

Black mane of hair
falling down,
brush of the hand
slicked back on the crown.

The Crow Brady – caw caw
The Crow Brady,
caw cawing his price,
playing it down.

Pre-ambling with:
'pigs are slow the year,
caw caw,
aye pigs are slow the year
but never fear, Crow Brady,
aye the Crow is here'

'The pigs are the only things that
are slow then,' my mother would say.

'Ah ya never lost it mam.'

'Never had it to begin with.'

Then the Crow would dance around,
price tags falling from his mouth.

'You'll take this.'

'I won't.'

'You'll take that.'

'I won't'.

'You'll end up with nothing –
me last word'.

'I'd drown them first'.

'Ya drive a hard bargain
Mrs Connerty'.

'You drive a big car, Mr. Brady'.

The intimacy of the deal would play
itself out along these lines.

'You'll take what I have in me
hand for the twelve of them'.
(Crow's laser eye on the litter)

'Depends on the size of your claw.'

'Any man 'id take it and be happy.'

'I'm not any man'.

Her eye was accustomed to judging the gain
by the aperture of the claw, his averted eye,
his see-saw disclosing shuffle, from side to side,
the feigned departure.

'We'll shake on it,' he'd rush,

'Shake on it, you'll be the death of me Crow Brady,'
she'd say taking the money,
'the death of me and half the country'
(she could feign it too.)

'The death! The death of you and
half the country.  Amn't I keeping
yez all alive, Mrs Connerty.'

Caw, Caw and off he'd go,
high tailing it out the gate.

'I'll be back for the 12 tomorrow.'

## 4.

### The Deal

And the next day,
the Crow Brady's driver would arrive.
Horizontal laths on a lowered tailboard
for the hoof grip.
Litter and skitter,
their genuflected falls,
up onto a trailer.

That night in the bar,
big black boot on a stool.

'I'm no man's fool ya know,
no man's fool'

He puffed about the bargain,
got them for a song
he would sing,
and the boom of his voice
around the bar it would ring.

Next day he arrived and
he crowed and he crowed.
The mother slipped in a runt,
one short of a load,
one short of a load.

Caw Caw

# THE CROW FAMILY

## Raven

The black raven nestles high,
sings, as good as any,
to the night sky,
the alchemy of things to come,
sluicing water from a pump,
on the village square and the tumbleweed
of footfalls to a Dispensary door.

## Magpie

Exocet eye,
dead eyeing us,
fantail, free fall, flight,
we calibrate our well being
by your numbers.
And our progeny and wealth
is tied up in the sorcery
of secrets you withold.

# SCARS ON THE LAND

# BACKBONE

*"It steadies me to tell these things"*
(from Squarings 32, *Seeing Things* by Seamus Heaney

## 1

More than a metaphor for a Burren Park,
these stony sea pictures
of my backbone,
MRI cave paintings.

More than a soundtrack –
"Where Corals Lie"
playing in my ears,
to allay the fears of

hemmed in,
strafing magnets,
pummelling protons, knocking me
off frequency.

## 2

An organised band of weather,
on a Gulf Stream,
coming in off the Atlantic.
Precipitation,

peppering the land,
raining down with a sculptor's hand
hammer and chisel
pelt and peal and pull.

And stone gives way
to the siege,
slow dissolving time.

Osteoporosis of limestone
yields
to the weight of water.

Clint and gryke,
paving the way,
stepping stones of the soul.

The wind out here
would rattle you,
if you were on your own.

And yet being on your own
and being alone
and listening to

the delirium of air
is all there is
to steady you.


3

*Uisce faoi thalamh*

Fissure of gryke
and the bottleneck-glug
of gargoyle-gargling water.

Runnels of rain,
anterograde flow
through sphincters of light.

Hidden rivers coursing
in veins and arteries
under the skin.

Bone and stone
are only skin deep,
kin deep.

Exfoliating
dissolving, absolving,
shedding light,

on this border,
where drumlines are written,
beating out the bardo,

liminal lines between
what's seen above,
hidden below.


4

The Burren song sings
to "Where Corals Lie"

inwards
and
downwards.

Symphony of stone,
ad lib of flood waters

in the dark cave,
making it hard to say

who's calling.

# RETURN
*i.m. of Richard Morgan*

Salmon

> You leave wake lines, trailing behind you…
> Your imprint in water, frenzied bubbles…
> an epistaxis of bloodlines, from your exertions.
>
> No one was to know how far you came,
> how hard you swam against the current,
> to return home to the same stream,
> where you were born.

Clay

> The ferryman, Mogue, ferries you
> across Templeport lake to your final resting place,
> and on the island you are scattered to the wind,
> amongst the living and the dead.
>
> And the weaver is on the selvage now,
> out on the very edge of the fabric
> of your beginning and end.
>
> Ashes to ashes, clay to clay,
> opened ground, opening the way of Mogue,
> and Killian, blessing this new found land,
> where Eithne stands sentinel,
> a hazel-wood staff flowering, in her hand.
>
> We leave you, Richard, now on sacred ground
> and the sanctuary and seal we found,
> we carry with us now, as a talisman and more,
> on a bobbing boat to a shore,
> of memory; joy, sadness, thanksgiving.

Cuckoo

> From the thicket the birdsong swells,
> and at a certain point in the chorus,
> you can hear a steady-metronome refrain,
> cuckoo announcing,
> the arrival of summer again.

## REMEMBERING THE HOUSE GOING UP

Past midnight the house
loosens its foundations,
its grip on the earth,
that remembers trenches,

dug in a barren field,
dry as a bone when the sun shone,
flooded, when the skies opened.
A maze, a warren

and the space between,
not big enough, it seemed,
to the unpractised eye,
to house much.

But when the walls went up,
a grazing patch becomes a room,
a path through the fields,
a corridor.

Everything closes in.
The roof keeps a lid on it.
Enclosed ground,
sees the sun and moon no more.

# EMPTY DWELLINGS

## 1
## Vacant Lot

Title deeds to a gavel coming
down on going, going, gone.

Forty five acres of real estate
host like, ghost like,

intestate,
no will in the world to live.

They promised the melodies
of songbirds, larks ascending

and all that jazz.
A hoarding lies sideways on a heap,

an east wind scours, whips at the gloss,
rain washes big words away.

Crow, from his crow's nest,
surveys the vacant lot,

reads between the lines,
the cause and the effect not lost on him.

House lights don't light,
the village seems remote,

a show house, still in full dressage,
draperies of doilies,
velvety curtains,
fal-di-dahs.

DRAWING ON MEMORY

**2**
**Intestines**

A JCB hangs its head to the ground.
The mixer's mouth is frozen.
Dried mortar chokes the gills.

No engine putters to a start,
no saw sisses through wood grain,
the claw-hammer loses its grip,
hedges grow higher, verges greener,
rain finds its own way to the water course.

Houses avenue and crescent their way to incompleteness,
the grey pallor fixes for the need of sun,
and black ties between inner and outer blocks,
heavy with mortar,
bring the dampness in.

No headgear on the dwellings,
save black-felt scarves,
2 by 1 hairpin laths,
holding the whole thing
down.

Inside a hot press immersed
in news of hot and cold feeds –
unconnected.
Allen keys bleeding
the system dry.

Funiculus of wires hang.
Intestines, like rainbows,
cascading from a wall,
charged for a fuse board,
that hasn't arrived.
Trip switch names for inside rooms
fade and blur.

Birds lattice chimney pots
with the makings of nests
and chimney breasts
have lost the heart for fire.

With shell and cavity the wind plays
a hollow tune, then dies down.

An architrave of silence hangs
on the herringbone roofs,
a gable end looks out on unworked fields
– crochet of fallen wheat
– and the stalk of the eyes in corn.

# Rogue Garland

Beguiling ivy,
comfort blanket for feet at first,
duck down duvet of delight.

Meandering fingers,
tracing and lacing a triumphant
snuggery frill,

suckering its way
along calf and thigh,
midriff, cleavage and limb.

Squeeze-blouse tight,
circling round and round,
bringing everything to a head.

Dizzy canopy,
rogue garland of desire,
tightens its grip.

Tiara of tentacles,
necklace of ivy,
ash breath taken clean away.

# A Man By The Water At 6am

Like a stork he appeared,
in the Dodder stream,

his white shirt, winnowing
in his hand, above his head,

as he peeled off his layers
to take the waters in,

a shock of red hair,
a feral fox,

hands and knees on the rocks,
an otter pawing water on a stone,

the errant movement of his head,
the wayward look,

up and downstream,
his bicycle above him, on the river bank

leaning against a lone tree,
going nowhere.

## ASTRAY

That Fiachra left the pork chop,
untouched on the plate
and had a coal fire burning  on
a mild enough day in spring,
was not in itself  peculiar.

Nor indeed the fact that the paling posts,
out front, were painted green, white and gold
the day before, as he had been given to such activities,
of late, since he returned home from Mullingar,
with no one now to look out for him.

More the fact that the Massey Ferguson was
still running on the street and
the link box was lifted up, at a tilt,
with a pick, shovel and crowbar
ready for some dig

or set for fencing the lower field,
but no stakes in sight.

Out in the yard
diesel fumes filled the air.
Cars roared on the by pass nearby.

Everyone in the village had their say and more.

Goldie, the retriever wasn't herself,
circling at an outhouse door.

## CUT LOOSE

*after Dennis O'Driscoll*

*'life's a long song*
*but the tune ends too soon for us all'*
                                    *– Jethro Tull*

Epitaph on an empty grave,
eulogy for the next internee,
the air uncoupled from its song,
plays itself out along these lines,
cut loose in the night when
the tethering to the here and now,
this world, is slackened.

Or by day
when curlew-printed arrows
in mud, point the way
of no return through the gap
between Polly's Field and the Nine Acre.

Last things,
the last play out,
of notes on the scale,
lightened by the coloratura
of not knowing that

the arc of bird wings in flight,
the hoar of frost,
eel grass shimmying in a sheugh,
the smell of woodsmoke rising,
the drone of a milking parlour
in the distance,

were last things to be seen
and sensed and heard,
on a day that was remarkably
no different than any other.

# Requiem

*Open up the Holy Books,*
*let the annals of the secular impart,*
*your blunted instruments, chapter and verse*
*to repair this broken heart.*

What to do with this opened wound,
pulsing, like breath coursing through me,
last thing before I sleep,
first thing when I wake,

ghost limb of grief,
severed, missing,
everywhere the fragrant,
yet pungent
ardour of gone.

Who will write the requiem,
sing 'dirges in the dark',
in these dark days,
that come and go,
illuminated by light,
heated by the sun?

We fall on our wintering ways.
Shutters are drawn.
Lockdown and retreat,
we sit with the vacant lot,
document the disappeared.

## MUSEUM OF LOST MEMORY

*for Jane and Joe*

In the Museum of Lost Memory
forgetting is the key.

And unravelling the interrogatives of:
where and when did all this forgetting begin?
How and why did it happen?
And whose story is untold?

Leads us to the locker room
of the hurt,
the set aside,
the forgotten,

buried alive
in the coward's words of;
'time to move on,
there was hurt on all sides'.

And the door to the undocumented,
the disappeared, rises up.
And the key to it is in the...
wait now, 'til I remember...

Yes, under that potted plant,
no, under the doormat,
or did they say it was in the bed
beside the forget-me-nots?

No, for the life of me
I cannot remember, they say.
And 'cannot remember' becomes the mantra,
the escape route, the get-out clause.

But the key is in the front door,
where it has been, all the time.

Anticlockwise the turn.

Let yourself out too,
let yourself out of all recollections.

For you, like so many others,
have been knocking from the inside all along.

# SCARS

*'toute blesseur doit manger sa douleur'*

Two cat's eyes, faded scars
on my left calf.
A cyclops or sphynx on my right.

The white of the eye, set in
the penumbra of my pyoderma gangrenosum,
the man-eating flesh fissure
that swallowed grief,

burrowed deep, full as a tick
on sorrow, the inescapable way-of-it-is-like
leaving that had not been planned

on his 'Mirror in February' day
when he could hold no more
of what he had seen.

He had wind rush in his veins,
shifting clouds in his eyes,
limbs and joints overstretched

by what he had felt, tasted,
sensed, on the other side of knowing.
The not-safe-here alarm sounded,

his exit strategy, away from me,
back to a holding place,
a nest with high rims.

*'and every wound must
swallow its own pain'*

and so, I to mine,
to an emptying house
of his scent, his music, his sound.

In the white of the faded scar,
an eye slit is milking over,
like the soothsayers,

like Tiresias, looking out over Thebes,
blind and declaiming,
'I know what sickness haunts our city'.

## ISLAND OF THE ANNALEE

The disappearing island
has gone to ground,
a slow death by drowning,
in the constant stream
of rushing water,
churned-up pebbles,
sediment, stones,

chipping away,
perch by perch,
undertow and swirl,
under slithery roots
of sally and ash
losing their foothold,
nodding descent, acquiescence to the wind,

but the weight of outlier you carry,
around your neck,
burdensome and lonely,
you turn around,
transform, as anchor,
steely-rooted grip tight
hold on the river bed.

This is land worth fighting for.
This is land where salmon and pike
can lie down together in eelgrass,
knowing that the bed they make, spawns

fish who can fathom the deep,
who will journey out far
beyond the riptide
and return.

## STILL LIFE

*i.m. of Kathleen Conaty 1919-1982*

You carried your name on a wristband,
plastic tubes, your living arteries.
You lay still.
No camera could hold your frame so still.

You were beyond words,
without the heart to feel,
without the breath to speak.
Your low tide revealed

a cry beneath white porcelain skin,
a lament for left luggage,
the felony in the unfulfilled.
Heave deep and breathe mother,

blow out blocked tubes of ancestors past.
Feel again and touch and see and sing,
so that we can see you once again,
as you once were.

# DRAWING UP A LIST OF NOUNS – THE NAMES FOR LOVE

# Heart Of The Matter

*for Jac*

High pressure came in.

With a winter sun
low in the sky,
it was hard to see
what was happening ahead.

They sent a probe,
into the very heart
of the matter.

The scan picked up
a flower,

that had not been named,

that had not been seen before.

# Love In A Time Of Covid

*for Jac and John*

In Covid there's Ovid.
In Ovid, a void,
where Metamorphoses begins
and the particles of change
collide.

From chaos and darkness,
to order and light,
shafting through a crack,
in a party wall,
between two lovers,

Pyramus and Thisbe,　distanced,
but each to the other whispering,
intimacies of the flesh,
the heart.

And though apart,

their words move through stone
to the cupped-inner ear,
reverberating
on oscillating bone.

The longed-for embrace,
contours of contact,
an audible trace of sigh and sound
they hold each other,

as they lie on separate ground.

Scaling heights,
they come together, consummate,
desires of the heart,
that no wall can separate.

　　　　　　　　DRAWING ON MEMORY

# A Time To Leave Things Be

**1.**

Coming towards the end
there's a time to leave things be:
the rake to its missing teeth,
the graip to a twisted tine
and the ball of twine to its knotted self,
past the point of binding anything, any more.

Fragments of lives
fleet in and out.
Memory, the cause
can barely summon up
a subordinate clause to rally again.
We loiter without intent,
desire heads for the back door.

**2.**

When everything is taken away
what's left then?
An inhalation of air,
an exhalation of despair.

**3.**

And yet we breathe on,
gasp alone,
turned to the prone position,
we heave, lunge for air
and countering despair,
the ventilator sucks and blows in unison,

like bellows to a fire,
at which we sit,
marshalling all the wind there is,
to keep her lit.

# FLIGHT

*for Kim*

When Cupid draws back his bow,
all hell breaks loose.

He knows the pincer grip
and the soft touch
of feather flight,
the tightening of the string
into the slit
and the arrow head
lengthening its promise.

The slow bent elbow
and the slipped release,

the crease
in a black dress,
pleated,
a detail,
picked up by the archer's eye.

## FISHERMAN
*for Michael Walshe*

The mayfly will soon be up
on the Annalee,
and you will see him again,
in his waders,
knee-deep in water,

scribbling the air with his
cast of butterflies, dragonflies,
damselflies.  The fecundity of flight
all around him, lifting
the possibility of a catch higher

into the air, the lasso of the line
taken by the stream, past rock pool,
over eelgrass and lichen on rocks,
one side of the dissolving island
to the tail of the race,

where the float rests,
nesting on the meniscus
of water,

bobbing, nosing,
then up tailing,
giving up its buoyancy
to something
              tugging
                     from
                           the deep.

## MASTERCLASS
*for Hubert Conaty*

On Fridays, the Master would lower the whole world
down on a map, for all of us to see.

From the question-mark hook, he uncoiled the cord,
brought it down to earth from its high perch.

As he loosened his grip, the South Pole hurtled
into free fall onto the chalk ledge.

I watched Australia, New Zealand, Antartica disappear
in accordion folds of blue,
seismic waves swelling, tectonic plates shifting and

swallowing up the names of islands, I'd not heard of before.
I rolled them out on my tongue, to hear
the sounds of far away places;

Vanuatu, Tuvalu, Fiji,
Tonga, Tristan Da Cunha, Réunion and Easter

rising again like the outstretched hand
of the Master, that calms the storm.

I can see him still as
he takes the strain of the rope, feels the tug,
lifts the mainsail smooth again.

We embark on vast oceans, deserts, an endless sky,
eyes level with the equator
we stand, high on a world

that opens and turns...

## DUENDE
*for Finn*

You have discovered a new piece
of music, a new song to throw yourself into.

And you literally do –
fling yourself on the floor.

High pitch and low pitch,
you call out to me to come and listen.

My solitary presence,
your audience of thousands.

You lure me into your net,
mixing flailing arms with pirouettes,

and entrechats, spring heeled you hit the air,
punch out, each note taking you higher and higher.

You lift a crutch I use for walking,
the handle becomes a microphone,

and the loop for my upper arm, a camera
that follows you all around the stage.

You are perfectly lost, releasing yourself
to the song,
abandoning yourself
to the very air of things.

## Moving On
*for Davin*

You've discovered the gym,
every sinew and muscle
that you meticulously research,
you hone, fine tune,
make strong.

I can see you on
a Grecian postcard from the past,
a man of Aran,
strong under a currach
being launched to sea.

Your foothold giving way
in sand,
filling with sea-water,
emptying, subsiding,

as you take on the tide,
release yourself to it.

## No Looking Back

*for Kim*

Your hair, fanning out,
like eelgrass in water.

Your action strong.
heel to heel,
thrusting for fluid movement.

Your hands imprinting water
with your palms
and your arms opening

in a breast stroke,
like the opening of the arms
in a diva's encore.

Song bubbles, trailing from your mouth.
Notes scaling the depths with
your airs, your graces.

And I am watching over you now
my love. Sleep well
and hold the deep.

For you have travelled there,
and down there in the deep
I first met you.

Orpheus and Eurydice,
no looking back
my love,

no looking back.

## SKINNY'S YOUR ONLY MAN

*for the three sisters.*

Skinny's your only man
and the only God we prayed to,
when we tried to get
the skinny jeans on.

Slipping feet into stretchies,
pulling past ankle,
wriggling past knees and arse,
then flopping onto the bed.

Cheek-to-cheek suck in,
the well positioned hook of
the wire hanger ready to go
into the zip hole
and whoosh...sealed.

The last manoeuvre
to get up,
a sideways swivel
to the edge of the bed.

No room to tuck in the blouse,
just about enough scope for locomotion
when you're poured in,
(which she was reminded of,
time and again, before leaving.)

The night was hers.
How could she fit in a few pints, she thought.

More to the point, though,
what in the name of God would she do
if she got lucky?

## SOPHIA GRACE

*"It is your time now, time to hear your voice*
*in a world gone silent, waiting for the sound of hope."*

No one was expecting you Sophia, till Christmas.
You arrived before your time, in mid-November, into a world,
coming and going, coming and going,
too busy to notice the tremor,
the quake of your arrival.

Favourable winds brought you here
and favourable winds will carry you on.
"You came by old roads,
to open new ones".

Your breath is soft and still,
like a rainforest mist,
settling over a Coolatty hill.
And the breast you fondly nurse upon,
could be teeming waters
from the sacred Amazon.

Wisdom is written in your name, Sophia.
The star in the east cannot hold a candle
to the light in your eyes, a star,
that wise women from the South followed
and came to you from afar.

And you have Grace in your movement, supple feet,
those legs of yours kicking up a samba, to a Brazilian beat.
Heel to toe and toe to heel,
for the sake of balance,
you strike up an Irish reel.

No borders, *sem fronteirias*
between you and the rest of the world,
and all the barriers,
that you have taken down,
brings *carnaval, celebraçao,*

a southern star, to a northern town.

## SWALLOWS

*for Sean Conaty*

I was five, when I met you face to face,
wrapped up in a warm cocoon,
high up in the rafters of a forge,
one late afternoon.

Your eyes fixed on me,
mine looked into yours
and I could feel
your wings beat.

A flap, a flutter,
a faltering rise,
over the edge
and out to the skies.

Your altimeter needle wavered,
your flight plan, askew,
your body possessed
by everything new.

You fell in love
with the air itself,
took it in,
let it lift you up,

to new heights.
Warm air currents,
prevailing winds,
your comrades in arms.

You mastered the rise,
you mastered the fall,
you learned the steady course.
You listened to the call,

to lead,
to fall into line,
to release yourself to the airflow,
when weather was fine.

Fledglings,
fork-tailed arrows of hope,
pointing the way.
A congregation of faith in flight,

bob and balance, murmuring
mantras of lift off and leave,
whispering prayers
of hope and return.

I saw your lines
on the telegraph wires,
your lines,
my first long poem,

calling me
to come and fly,
to take
the long way home.

## ACKNOWLEDGEMENTS

Acknowledgements are due to the editors of the following where some of these poems, or versions of them, have been published:

Windows Anthology (Eds. Noel Monahan, Heather Brett)
Doghouse Anthology (Ed. Noel King)
Off the Leash, Field Notes (Otherworld Press, Seamus Cashman)
Cuilcagh Lakelands UNESCO Global Geopark – Digital Poetry Map, funded by Geological Survey Ireland, (Ed. Bee Smith)
Probe, C.B. Quartreman, (Bregazzi, Bradish, Cashman & Conaty) (Otherworld Press).
Celebration of Literature, Droimin Creatives, in association with Arts Council (Ed. Heather Brett)

Commissioned Poems for Public Art Projects:
"Ballyhaise Framed", Dr. Anne Burke, Cavan Co. Council
"In the Current", Yvonne Cullivan , Cavan Co. Council

The Compass Project (Comhlamh)

Tyrone Guthrie Centre, Annamakerrig, Newbliss, County Monaghan

Cover image, *Liminal Landscape,* Emma Finucane.

Dublin South F.M., where some of these poems were broadcast.

Thanks is due to my editor Dominic Taylor for his faith in the poems and to Revival Press, Limerick for publishing the collection.

To Chris Binchy, Noel Monahan and Mary O'Donnell for their insight, encouragement and comments.

To my fellow collaborators in the collective – C.B. Quarterman – Daragh Bradish, Paul Bregazzi and Seamus Cashman for their helpful responses to some of these poems.

To Seamus Cashman, at Otherworld Press, for his support and bringing many creative projects to print.

A special thanks to Catriona O'Reilly and all the staff at The Cavan Arts Office for the many years of support and recognition of the work and facilitating the bringing of this collection to fruition and attention of the public.

To Joe Keenan and Padraig McIntyre, Town Hall Theatre , Cavan for their pragmatism and advice.

Thanks to Kim for her unwavering support and honesty and to Zoe and herself for the typing and retyping the many drafts of these poems.

Thanks to Ciana Campbell for her help and encouragment.

Thanks to my colleagues, the children and parents at Zion Parish Primary School and all the schools I have taught in for keeping the spark alive by supporting and participating in the many creative arts projects over the years.

Thanks to Paul Bregazzi and Seosamh Ó Cuinneagáinn for proofreading.

# NOTES

*Duet on a Manuscript*
"glossolalia" – speaking in tongues, utterances approximating words and speech – the tongue moves, in many cases without the conscious control of the speaker.

*First Thing This Morning*
"a little silver slipper of a moon" – The Glass Menagerie, T. Williams

*Field Notes*, is a response to "In the Current" (Yvonne Cullivan), a public art project, commissioned by Cavan Arts Office in 2013, under the Per Cent for Art Scheme, and funded by the Dept. of the Environment, Community and Local Government and the National Roads Authority. The commission was particular to Belturbet Town, Co. Cavan, Ireland.
Yvonne Cullivan is a multidisciplinary visual artist, educator and creative consultant based in Galway city, in the west of Ireland.
Further information see www.yvonnecullivan.info.
Original music for Field Notes composed by Finn Conaty.
(The Putiaghans are an imagined people, who lived in the townland of Putiaghan, near Belturbet, where a bronze age settlement was evident).

*Underwriter*
*Variations on lines by Seamus Heaney*
"the sky at the bottom of the well" – ref to The Wellhead
"into the marvellous" – "Out of the Marvellous" from Lightenings VIII
"Sing us to where the singing comes from" – "sing yourself to where the singing comes from" The Wellhead

*Burying the Compass*
Commissioned poem for the winding down and incorporation of the NGO development education organisation Compass into Comhlamh

*Appetite*
"sensilla" – Zoology term for sensory receptors, typically hair

*Lasting Impression*
A "last" is a mechanical form shaped like a human foot, used by shoemakers and cobblers in the manufacture and repair of shoes.

*Breaking the Bread*
(i) Selected lines from the Stabat Mater – A 13th century Christian hymn to Mary, mother of Jesus, portraying her suffering at his crucifixion.
Stabat mater dolorosa (the sorrowful mother stood)
O quam tristis et afflicta (oh how sad and stricken)
Eloi, Eloi lama sabachtani (my God, my God, why have you forsaken me?)
Jesus' last words before he died.
(ii) Norbertine Order founded 900 years ago in Prémoutré in France by St. Norbert of Xanten. They had an abbey in Kilnacrot, Cavan.
The names in section 1, Bean Uí Luanaigh and Fr. Boyle are entirely fictitious.

*Pigs Suite*
"dressing the pigs" – a term that was used in some Northern Counties, as a euphemism, for the castration of young male pigs.

*Backbone*
Selected poem for Cuilcagh Lakelands UNESCO Global Geopark – Digital Poetry Map

*Return*
"epistaxis" – a medical term for nosebleeds
(The section Clay is prompted by the story of St. Mogue's Island)

*Museum of Lost Memory*
The Disappeared Commission in Northern Ireland , a National Library of Ireland open invitation for submissions to inform its National Collections policy and the work "Museum of Broken Things" by artist Jane McCormack prompted this poem. Concluding lines in homage to J. Rumi, 13th c Sufi poet.

*Scars*
(i) "toute blesseur doit manger sa douleur" – Bernard Noël from Le Reste d'un Poeme (The Remnant of a Poem), "every wound must swallow its own pain".

This poem was translated by Michael Brophy, on the occasion of Bernard Noël's visit toIreland for "Vendanges Poétiques, a bi-lingual festival of poetry, Dublin 2004.
(ii) "Mirror in February" – a poem by Thomas Kinsella

(iii) "I know what sickness haunts our city" – prompted by lines spoken by Oedipus to Tiresias, the blind prophet.(Oedipus Rex, Sophocles)

*Island on the Annalee*
After "Annaghelee", a print by Holger Christian Lőnze's, Ballyhaise Framed (Dr. Anne Burke), commissioned and curated Cavan County Arts Office under the Percent for Arts Scheme, published by Cumann Seanchais Bhréifne.

# ENDORSEMENTS FOR DRAWING ON MEMORY BY TOM CONATY

*Drawing on Memory*, is a consistent and thoughtful book of poetry drawn from Tom Conaty's unique investigative skills into the meaning of life.

*– Noel Monahan*

In *Drawing on Memory,* Tom Conaty considers how we are shaped, coloured and haunted by experience. The voice is clear and intimate. His attention is unfailing. Boundaries are fuzzy and strangeness is always close. The dead come back to life, animals assume control, relationships bloom and fade, lines are redrawn on maps, words take on new meaning, names almost forgotten. The border between the real and the imagined blurs. This is a collection that deals with the consequences of the past, and takes glorious pleasure in the tiny moments that we can't shake off.

*– Chris Binchy*

Tom Conaty's poems are rich, controlled and very beautiful. The poet probes cartographies of a sacred land, and the position of humans in such ancient places. Certain poems – earthy, instinctual – show the poet drawing on word-hoards of memory, setting them ablaze in a fluid past or present, bringing to our attention a soothsayer, a man stripping off in the river Dodder, a suicide. He also writes of love – absent, abused, and passionate. The subject of the powerful poem Breaking the Bread of Life – A Communion Sequence, is clerical crime and child abuse, the tone understated but accusatory. The phenomenal world of crow, magpie and corncrake, is particular and vivid while the tremulous capacity of Border Fox reminds the reader of ungodly political terror in other times. Like so many poems in this luminous collection, it brims with grace, grit, and subtle vision. Tom Conaty's poetry is simply revelatory and I loved this collection.

*– Mary O'Donnell*

# About Revival Press

*"A good poem shocks us awake, one way or another - through its beauty,
its insight, its music; it shakes or seduces the reader out of the common
gaze and into a genuine looking. And make no mistake I consider such a
moment of transformation to be a radical event."*

— *Jane Hirshfield*

Revival Press is a community publishing press and is the poetry imprint of
The Limerick Writers' Centre. It was founded by managing editor Dominic
Taylor in 2007. It grew out of the Revival Poetry Readings established in
Limerick 2003 by Barney Sheehan and Dominic Taylor. It has published over
fifty poetry titles to date.

Revival has also helped establish a number of local and national poets by
publishing their first collections.

One of the aims of Revival Press is to make writing and publishing both
available and accessible to all. It tries as much as possible to represent diverse
voices and advocates for increased writing and publishing access to individuals
and groups that have not typically had this access.
It continues to represent local authors and to offer advice and encouragement
to aspiring writers.

Revival Press supports Fair Trade Publishing.